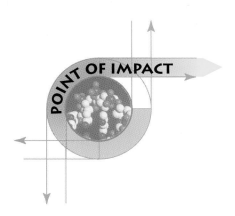

POINT OF IMPACT

Understanding DNA

A Breakthrough in Medicine

TONY ALLAN

Heinemann Library
Chicago, Illinois

Produced for Heinemann Library by Discovery Books Limited
Designed by Ian Winton
Illustrations by Stefan Chabluk
Originated by Ambassador Litho Limited
Printed in Hong Kong

06 05 04 03 02
10 9 8 7 6 5 4 3 2 1

Library of Congress Cataloging-in-Publication Data
Allan, Tony, 1946-
    Understanding DNA : a breakthrough in medicine / Tony Allan.
        p. cm. -- (Point of impact)
Includes bibliographical references and index.
Summary: Examines the events and circumstances leading to the discovery of DNA and the impact of this discovery on the scientific and medical communities.
    ISBN 1-58810-557-1 (lib. bdg.)   ISBN 1-4034-0074-1 (pbk. bdg.)
    1. DNA--History--Juvenile literature. [1. DNA--History. 2. Genetics--History.] I. Title. II. Series.
    QP624 .A42 2002
    572.8'6'09--dc21

                                    2001003481

Acknowledgments
The author and publishers are grateful to the following for permission to reproduce copyright material:
A. Barrington Brown/Science Photo Library, pp. 4, 16; Danny Lehman/Corbis, p. 5; Hulton Archive, p. 6; Popperfoto, p. 7; Hulton Getty, p. 8; Hulton Deutsch, p. 10; BBC Hulton Picture Library, p. 12; J. C. Revy/Science Photo Library, p. 13; Bettmann/Corbis, pp. 14, 15; Science Source/Science Photo Library, p. 17; King's College Archives, p. 19; Wellcome Institute, pp. 20, 24; Laurent H. Americain/Science Photo Library, p. 21; Sue Ford/Science Photo Library, p. 22; James King Holmes/Science Photo Library, p. 23; Maximilian Stock/Science Photo Library, p. 25; Popperfoto/Reuters pp. 26, 28; Chris Knapton/Science Photo Library, p. 27; Stevie Grand/Science Photo Library, p. 29.

Cover photographs reproduced with permission of: A. Barrington Brown/Science Photo Library (top); Maximilian Stock/Science Photo Library (bottom).

Every effort has been made to contact copyright holders of any material reproduced in this book. Any omissions will be rectified in subsequent printings if notice is given to the publisher.

Some words are shown in bold, **like this.** You can find out what they mean by looking in the glossary.

Contents

The Secret of Life

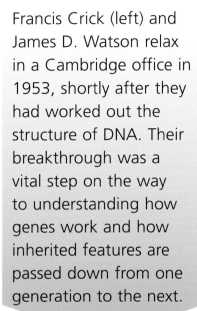

Cambridge, England, 1953

Regular customers at the Eagle restaurant in the university town of Cambridge were used to the two scientists from the nearby Cavendish Laboratory who came in at lunchtime most Saturdays. They talked loudly and had many friends. One was a big, jovial Englishman in his thirties, the other was a younger American. That particular day in March 1953, they seemed more talkative than usual. The Englishman was telling anyone who cared to listen about a breakthrough the two had just made, and what he was saying seemed unbelievable: He was claiming they had discovered the secret of life.

The mystery of the genes

The Englishman was Francis Crick, the American was James D. Watson, and the amazing thing about their claim was that it was true. They had unlocked the mystery of **genes** by discovering the structure of **DNA.** Genes were the key to **heredity:** the passing on of characteristics from one generation to the next, like red hair and brown eyes and some personality traits. Genes could even determine the likelihood of catching certain diseases. More than that, genes separated the species: they made tapeworms breed tapeworms, chimps have little chimps, and people have human babies.

Francis Crick (left) and James D. Watson relax in a Cambridge office in 1953, shortly after they had worked out the structure of DNA. Their breakthrough was a vital step on the way to understanding how genes work and how inherited features are passed down from one generation to the next.

An important discovery

Before Crick and Watson's discovery, there had been a huge obstacle blocking all clear understanding of how heredity worked. No progress could be made until people understood what exactly DNA was and the form it took—how the chemicals it was made of fit together. That was the mystery that the pair had finally cracked. It was a discovery that, nine years later, was to win them the **Nobel Prize** for Medicine. It was also the latest in a series of breakthroughs in the understanding of genes that another Nobel prizewinner, the French biochemist Jacques Monod, was to call "without any doubt the most important discoveries ever made in biology."

A group photo shows how similar features reappear in three generations of a Central American family, from grandmother down to infant. Besides affecting physical appearance, genes also help to shape a person's overall health.

THE GREATEST MOMENT

In his book *Genome*, science writer Matt Ridley sums up the world of possibilities Crick and Watson's discovery has created for people today: *"I genuinely believe we are living through the greatest intellectual moment in history. Until now our human genes were an almost complete mystery. We will be the first generation to penetrate that mystery. We stand on the brink of great new answers, but, even more, of great new questions."*

Building Blocks of Life

It runs in the family

The mystery that Crick and Watson started to unravel in 1953 was one that had fascinated people for over 5,000 years.

Breeds of cattle like the British shorthorn did not develop naturally. Instead, they were produced over many centuries by mating bulls and cows with certain desirable features—a process called selective breeding. Shorthorn cattle like these were bred to be muscular for their beef and with short horns to make them safer for farmers to handle.

People had always known that some physical features were passed down from parents to their children, and that characteristics like red hair or blue eyes often ran in families. They knew too that **heredity** affected not just humans but also animals and plants.

From aurochs to dairy cow

From early times people have practiced **selective breeding.** In selective breeding, one chooses plants or animals with desirable characteristics and mates them to produce future generations in which those traits become more pronounced. It was the technique early humans used in the Middle East 10,000 years ago to turn the wild aurochs—a large, fearsome, big-horned creature—into the docile milk-cow we are familiar with today. Similarly, farmers used specially selected seeds to cultivate strains of wheat that were easier to harvest than the wild varieties.

Bloodline

Over the centuries people continued to use this practical knowledge to produce crops that were better, breeds of cows that yielded more milk, and faster racehorses. While they knew selective breeding worked, no one had any clear idea why. One popular theory was that the inheritance passed through the blood. Terms like *bloodstock* and *bloodline* are leftovers from that error. The real nature of heredity remained an unsolved mystery.

SELECTIVE BREEDING

One of the earliest benefits of selective breeding may have been in horse-riding. The first horses to be tamed, 5,000 years ago, were too small to carry adults and were probably only used for carrying loads. Over many generations, however, the largest stallions among the small horses were mated with the largest mares until eventually a breed arose that was strong enough to bear the weight of riders. This revolutionized the way people traveled.

Like physical features, some medical conditions can be passed down within families. Britain's Queen Victoria, shown here (center) with some of her many relatives, is thought to have carried a hereditary blood disorder called hemophilia. One of her sons suffered from it, and so did several of her grandsons.

Pioneer of Heredity

Experiments with pea plants

The first person to work out scientifically how **heredity** functioned was not a famous scientist. He was a monk

named Gregor Mendel who lived in a monastery in the middle of the nineteenth century in what is now the Czech Republic. Put to work in the monastery kitchen garden, he started **crossbreeding** pea plants, keeping careful handwritten notes of the results.

Mendel's findings seemed to run against common sense. Most people at the time thought that if a tall plant was crossed with a short one, the result would be something in between. Mendel learned, though, that the resulting plants—those of what he called the F_1 generation—were all either tall or short.

Mendel continued his experiments beyond that second crop, and what he found in the F_2 generation was more surprising still. If all of the second-generation plants had been tall, it seemed likely that the next generation of plants bred from them would also be tall, but they were not. They were mixed—some tall and some short—and the mixture followed a clear pattern: one short plant for every three that were tall.

The Austrian monk Gregor Mendel was the first person to discover how heredity works. He did his research in the monastery garden, studying how certain features were passed down from one generation of pea plants to the next.

The laws of heredity

It was a mystery, but Mendel correctly worked out what was happening. Each young plant inherited something determining whether it would be tall or short—Mendel called this a "factor"—from each parent—one part from the father, one from the mother. One factor was usually stronger; Mendel called it "dominant." The weaker factor, called "recessive," would also be passed on. It might turn up unexpectedly further down the line of heredity, maybe after one generation or even after more.

Mendel's factors are what we now call **genes,** and what he had learned about peas subsequently turned out to be true not just of plants but of animals and people too. The retiring monk in his monastery garden had taken the first big step on the path that led to Crick and Watson's discovery. He had started to unravel the mystery of heredity.

This simple diagram explains how a characteristic such as height is passed on from one generation to the next.

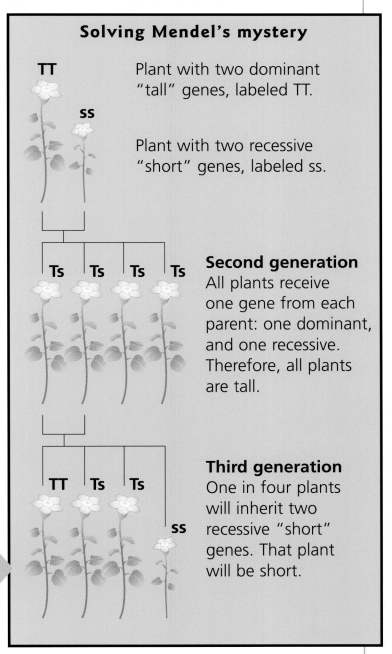

Solving Mendel's mystery

TT Plant with two dominant "tall" genes, labeled TT.

ss Plant with two recessive "short" genes, labeled ss.

Ts Ts Ts Ts

Second generation
All plants receive one gene from each parent: one dominant, and one recessive. Therefore, all plants are tall.

TT Ts Ts

ss

Third generation
One in four plants will inherit two recessive "short" genes. That plant will be short.

Seeing Small

Mendel rediscovered

Although Mendel had made a breakthrough, not many people knew about it at the time. As far as the scientific world was concerned, he was no more than a gardener. He published his findings in a little-read local journal where they failed to create a stir. Disillusioned, Mendel turned his attention instead to his monastery, becoming its head monk. His insights went unnoticed by most people.

That changed in 1900 when several scientists dusted off old copies of the journal and rediscovered his work. The reason for the new interest had nothing to do with peas or other plants. It had more to do with improvements in a scientific instrument that was already 200 years old in Mendel's day—the microscope.

Looking into the microscope

As better microscopes with more powerful lenses became available, scientists were able to study smaller and smaller objects. They had known for centuries that living things were made up of millions upon millions of tiny units called **cells.** Now they were able to peer into the cells themselves, and even into their innermost parts, the **nuclei.** What they saw there called to mind Mendel's factors, which after 1900 were given a new name: **genes.** By that time the race was on to find out what exactly genes might be.

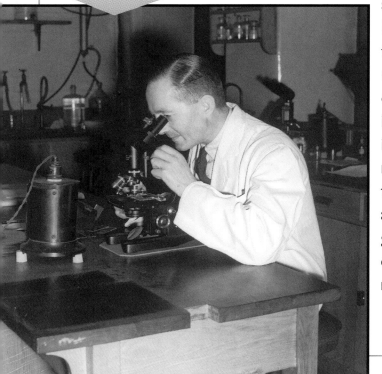

Microscopes allowed scientists to look inside cells, where the key to **heredity** ultimately lay. Instruments like this one can magnify up to 1,200 times.

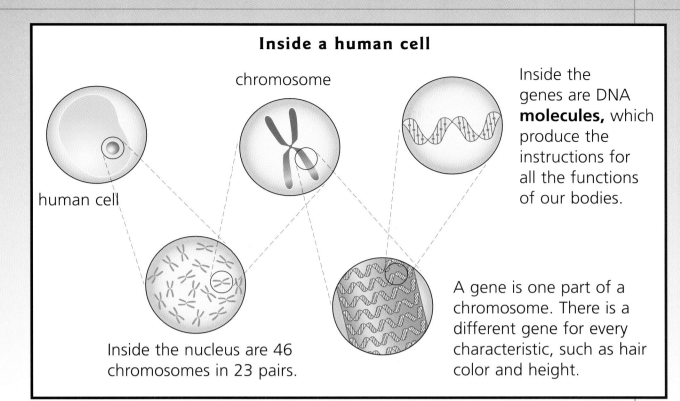

Inside a human cell

chromosome

human cell

Inside the nucleus are 46 chromosomes in 23 pairs.

Inside the genes are DNA **molecules,** which produce the instructions for all the functions of our bodies.

A gene is one part of a chromosome. There is a different gene for every characteristic, such as hair color and height.

Curiosity of the gene-hunters

For the most part the early gene-hunters had no idea where their research might lead or what benefits they would bring. Instead they were driven by curiosity and the urge to solve the mystery of how life passed from one generation to the next. The answer, they knew, must lie somewhere in the mysterious dots and squiggles of the microscopic world.

Scientists could now see that the nuclei of cells contained even smaller bodies within them. There were floating, rodlike shapes that turned red when stained with dye and so were called **chromosomes,** from "chroma," the Greek word for color. Chromosomes themselves were made up of something even smaller. As far back as 1869 a wispy microscopic thread had been noted by a researcher investigating pus-soaked bandages from a local hospital. In time, this wispy thread was recognized as **DNA.**

SECRETS OF THE CELLS

There are about 100 billion cells in the human body and in every one of them are 23 pairs of chromosomes. One half of each pair comes from the father, the other from the mother, and between them they make each of us the way we are, determining not just the way we look but also much of our personality.

A Momentous Meeting

Watson and Crick

James D. Watson was a child prodigy. He was accepted as a student by the University of Chicago when he was only fifteen. He was just 23 years old when he arrived, early in 1951, at the Cavendish Laboratory, Cambridge, where he met Francis Crick.

Francis Crick came from a very different background. He had studied physics at college, and then worked for the British Navy, designing mines for use in World War II. He had not turned to biology until 1947, and had so far done no significant work, but no one doubted his cleverness. Watson called him "the brightest person I had ever worked with."

It was here at Cavendish Laboratory, Cambridge, that the discovery of DNA's structure was made. Work done at King's College, London, by Maurice Wilkins and Rosalind Franklin was also vital in making the breakthrough possible.

DNA: The key to heredity

Both were already interested in **heredity** and how the instructions that shape all living things pass from one generation to the next. It was already understood by 1951 that it was **DNA**—the wispy thread seen only under the microscope—that passed on characteristics from one generation to the next, and that animals and plants each seemed to have their own special DNA. However, scientists did not understand how it happened. To unravel the mystery and discover the structure of DNA would involve both biology and chemistry.

At the time of their meeting, Crick was a relative beginner in biology; as for Watson, his background in chemistry had come to an early end as a student when he caused an explosion in a lab. As it turned out, what each of the two did know cancelled out what the other did not, and one of science's great partnerships was born.

King's College, London

In 1950 the center of research work on DNA was at King's College, London, not in Cambridge. Another problem for Crick and Watson was that individual pieces of DNA were too small to be seen even with the most powerful microscopes. The clearest images available came from **x-ray crystallography,** and these images were being produced at King's College. It soon became obvious to Crick and Watson that the path to the breakthrough they were seeking must lead through London.

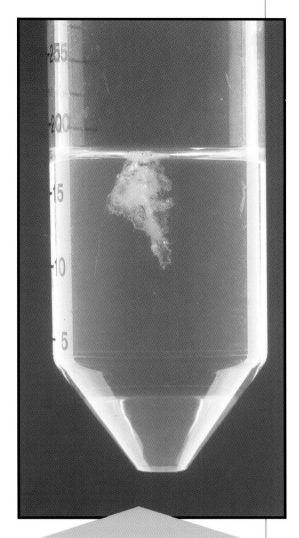

A quantity of DNA taken from white blood **cells** appears as a milky cloud in this magnified test-tube image. This sample would contain between 50,000 and 100,000 human genes.

X-RAY CRYSTALLOGRAPHY

X-ray crystallography was a technique with which people could take photographs of things too small to see even with the most powerful microscopes, including minuscule **proteins** and threads of DNA. Sadly, the results were anything but crystal clear; to most people they looked like fuzzy blurs. Yet a few farsighted individuals realized that within them lay the secret of the **genes**—and two of those people were Francis Crick and James Watson.

Rivals on the Trail

Wilkins and Franklin

As it happened, Watson had met the head of the King's College team, Maurice Wilkins, before he even arrived in Cambridge. Wilkins was a New Zealander, and it was seeing one of his images at a scientific conference that had originally gotten Watson excited about **DNA.**

The person with whom Wilkins worked most was Rosalind Franklin. She produced special photographs using a technique called **x-ray crystallography.** Her photographs provided the best clues to DNA's structure. When Franklin arranged a showing of her latest images in London, Watson went to see them. The pictures showed that DNA structure was a spiral, spun together from two to four chemical strands.

Born in New Zealand, Maurice Wilkins was the head of the King's College science team racing Crick and Watson to crack the code of DNA. He had trained as a physicist and, during World War II, had worked on the Manhattan Project, which produced the **atomic** bomb.

Watson was excited by the time he got back to Cambridge. The way forward, he felt, was to build a three-dimensional model of DNA, blown up in scale millions of times. This would show all the facts known about the various chemicals involved and how they might link up. That seemed to be the best way to find the right structure.

Making a model

Watson and Crick started on a three-strand model and were pleased with the results. They invited Wilkins and Franklin to come see it.

The visit was a disaster. Franklin was frustrated that other scientists were trying to explain her own research to her. She pointed out a basic error in their calculations and took the first train back to London. Word of the meeting reached the head of the Cavendish Laboratory, who officially warned Crick and Watson not to do any further work on DNA. He feared that his government-provided grant would be cut if his researchers were found to be working on problems already being investigated by Wilkins and Franklin.

The other rival that Crick and Watson most feared was Linus Pauling, the American chemist who was working on the DNA problem at California Institute of Technology (Cal Tech).

Competition from abroad

Crick and Watson were not easily discouraged, however. They felt a sense of urgency because they knew that, besides Wilkins and Franklin, another scientist was on the DNA trail. Linus Pauling, whom Watson once acknowledged as being "the greatest of all chemists," was working on the problem at his laboratory in California. He had already put forward a suggestion for a three-strand model. Now the partners heard that he was coming to London, where he would see Rosalind Franklin's most recent photos, which could only speed him along in his research. Crick and Watson had no time to lose if they were to keep ahead of the game.

Breakthrough!

More model-making

Crick and Watson went back to model-building. In the light of Franklin's comments, they made some basic changes to their designs. Previously they had put the chemical **bases** that were **DNA's** working ingredients on the outside of the main spiral that they had established in their model, but now they tried fitting them inside.

Linus Pauling never came to London, but when his son Peter arrived from the U.S. to study at Cambridge, Watson learned from him that Linus was back at work on DNA. Watson and Crick were delighted to learn that Pauling had made some mistakes. He still had the bases outside the spiral; worse yet, he had made a simple mistake in his chemistry.

James Watson looks on as Francis Crick explains the model they produced to illustrate DNA's structure. Knowing how the parts of DNA fit together was a step toward understanding how the messages that shape **heredity** are passed on.

Franklin's DNA photo

During another visit to London, Wilkins showed Watson Franklin's latest photo of a new form of DNA. It was the clearest image yet, and it seemed to confirm that Watson and Crick were on the right track. On the train back to Cambridge, Watson scribbled feverish calculations in the margin of his newspaper. By the time he went to bed that night he was convinced that DNA consisted of two strands interwoven in a spiral: a double **helix.**

Completing the puzzle

Much work remained to be done to show that the theory worked. Using metal plates produced in the laboratory's machine shops, Watson and Crick started making a model. At first nothing fit, so the pair tried an alternative approach, joining the chemicals together in a way they had not yet tried. This time everything slotted into place—the puzzle was complete. They had cracked DNA.

Here is part of a DNA **molecule** as shown by **x-ray crystallography.** By studying photos like this, Crick and Watson gained the insights that led to their breakthrough.

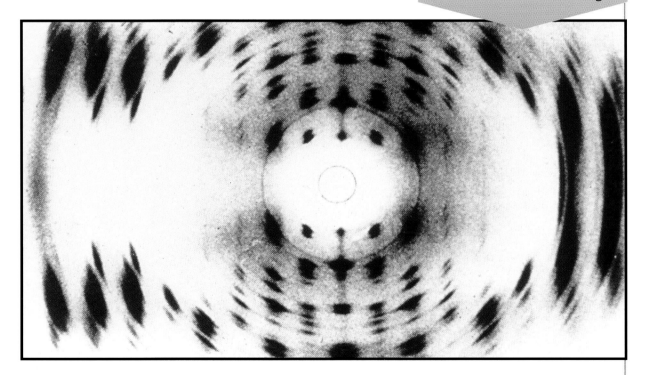

Telling the World

The staircase of life

The final model of the **DNA molecule** turned out to resemble a spiral staircase with each thread the same size and spaced at the same distance from the next. Crick and Watson had it ready to show to their colleagues by March 7, 1953, just five weeks after they had begun work on it.

Winners of the **Nobel Prize** for Medicine posed for a photograph after the 1962 awards ceremony in Stockholm, Sweden. Maurice Wilkins stands far left, Francis Crick is third from the left, and James Watson is second from the right.

Maurice Wilkins came up from London, and realized at once that the two had it right. They half expected him to be angry with them for stealing his data, but he was generous in his support, teasing them by writing, "I think you are a couple of old rogues. . . ." So, more surprisingly, was Rosalind Franklin; once the breakthrough had been made, her hostility toward the Cambridge duo vanished, to be replaced with mutual respect as both sides came to recognize the vital part the other had played in the achievement.

TO THE SUN AND BACK

If the DNA in a single human **cell** was unraveled into a single thread, it would stretch for 6 1/2 feet (2 meters). Together, all the DNA in all the cells in one person's body would be long enough to reach to the Sun and back many times.

Franklin not awarded Nobel Prize

Crick and Watson revealed their findings to the world in the journal *Nature,* in an article just 900 words long. Wilkins and Franklin also each published papers in the same issue so that their contribution would not be forgotten. It was not, and when Crick and Watson jointly received the Nobel Prize for their achievement nine years later, it was shared with a third person: Maurice Wilkins.

Rosalind Franklin died of cancer in 1958 at the age of 37, so she never got the recognition she deserved. Her notebooks showed that she too had narrowed the structure of DNA down to a double **helix** before her death.

The name that was missing was Rosalind Franklin's. Her photos had made the discovery possible, and it was only by a cruel trick of fate that her role was not formally recognized; she had died of cancer four years earlier. James Watson tried to make amends when he wrote a book called *The Double Helix,* noting that in time he and Crick "both came to appreciate greatly her personal honesty and generosity, realizing years too late the struggles that the intelligent woman faces to be accepted by a scientific world. . . ." It was an acknowledgement of their earlier misunderstandings, and it was no less than Rosalind Franklin's due, because her research had proved to be a turning point in their work.

Cracking the Genetic Code

Another beginning

However important the discovery of **DNA's** structure was to scientists at the time, it was to be several decades before it made any impact on the lives of ordinary people. For scientists, the discovery opened up a whole new world. For the first time scientists were able to explain exactly what **genes** are—stretches of DNA carrying the recipes to make **proteins,** the chemical building blocks of all life. Those proteins in turn can join together in billions of ways in different **cells.** All living things—plants, animals, and people—are formed from those cells.

DNA, it turned out, is a code that can be represented by just four letters: A, G, C, and T. These symbols identify the four chemicals—adenine, guanine, cytosine, and thymine—that make up DNA.

Millions of times larger than life-size, a model of DNA's structure reveals a pattern of two linked spirals twisting around one another. Crick and Watson called this "the double helix." In their model, the colored spheres represented separate **atoms.**

Inspired by Crick and Watson's insights, researchers started to look inside individual cells to find their chemical sequences. In the twelve years following the discovery of the double **helix,** scientists in many countries succeeded in working out how DNA operates. Crick and Watson both played an important part in this work of cracking the genetic code.

The birth of bioengineering

The next turning point came in the mid-1970s, when scientists learned how to transfer genes. They found a way of snipping pieces of DNA from one **chromosome** and then splicing them into another. Soon researchers were routinely shifting DNA from one plant to another and from animal to animal—sometimes even from animals to plants. In the beginning this work was done mainly by gene researchers trying to find out how genes worked, but the technique was quickly picked up by **biotechnology** companies. By 1983, 136 of the 383 U.S. companies using this technique were in the **pharmaceutical** industry.

This process became known as **bioengineering,** and it marked a huge step forward; it soon occurred to researchers that the new knowledge was opening up the instruction manual for life itself. Genetics would in the course of time reveal how all living things—snails as well as sea lions, daisies, and even people—are made, and through the techniques of bioengineering, scientists could take steps to alter the process.

This scientist is using a pipette to extract DNA from cells. Within 30 years of Crick and Watson's discovery, such techniques were becoming widespread in the science industry.

In Your Genes

Hopes for the future

Even though most of its benefits still lie in the future, **gene** research has opened up a whole new approach to health care, and it was for this reason that Crick, Watson, and Wilkins were awarded the **Nobel Prize** for Medicine. Its most obvious medical use lies in the treatment of **hereditary** diseases. There are over 4,000 known disorders caused by genetic problems, ranging from some types of deafness to fatal illnesses like Tay-Sachs disease, which kills most people born with it by the age of three. At the moment, only the symptoms of these conditions can be treated. The conditions cannot be cured.

Fighting hereditary diseases

Already scientists have been able to identify the defective genes responsible for a few hereditary conditions, such as some forms of **muscular dystrophy.** This has enabled them to devise tests that can show if a person is likely to pass the condition on to his or her children. Before these tests were available, people with family histories of such conditions had no way of knowing this. Knowing about these conditions could also help individuals change the way they live to reduce possible health risks.

A doctor examines a Jamaican boy suffering from sickle-cell disease. The condition, which stops the blood from functioning properly, is one of many caused by defects in the genes. Though genetics cannot yet cure these diseases, it can help identify parents at risk of passing them on to their children.

Why would people want to live their lives with a faulty gene, knowing that they could become ill at any time, if it could be avoided? Eventually, using genetic techniques, doctors may be able to go beyond treating the mere symptoms of disease. They may be able to get at the root cause of the disease: the faulty message in the genes that causes the body not to work properly in the first place. They may even be able to use **genetic engineering** techniques to replace faulty genes that could lead to fatal illnesses such as cancer.

The Human Genome Project

A vital step in making this genetic revolution possible is to find and list all of the genes that the human body contains. Thus, the Human Genome Project was launched—one of the biggest scientific undertakings ever—with, at the start, James Watson heading its U.S. branch. The aim of the Human Genome Project is to map every single gene and find out where it lies in the 23 pairs of **chromosomes** found in almost every **cell** of the human body. This will help scientists know where to look for specific traits, thereby enabling them to target specific diseases.

The project began in October 1990 and a first draft was completed in 2000. There turned out to be fewer genes than expected—about 30,000 to 35,000, rather than the 100,000 researchers had initially predicted.

A scientist working on the Human Genome Project watches as a robot camera displays images of bacteria containing human **DNA** on a television screen. The project, which was officially launched in 1990, has involved hundreds of scientists in at least eighteen countries.

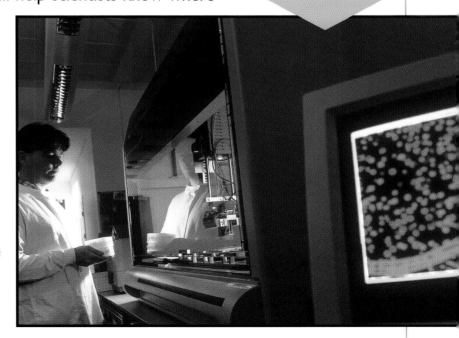

Advances in Medicine

Skin grafts

While many of the possible medical benefits lie in the distant future, some advances have already been made. Engineered human skin is being commercially produced by several **biotechnology** companies. Healthy **cells** taken from a donor are used to grow new skin. Although this product is not currently licensed for use in all countries, it is potentially helpful for treating people with serious burns. The only other treatment is to have skin grafted from other undamaged parts of the body, which is a more painful and complicated procedure.

Insulin used by diabetics can now be made to order in the laboratory using genetically engineered yeasts or bacteria.

Making medicines

More and more drugs are now being manufactured using the new techniques. In 1982, **genetically engineered** insulin, the drug used by **diabetics,** was approved for human use. Previously insulin was derived from cows and pigs, but now it can be produced in the laboratory.

Animals can be genetically modified to produce drugs that help treat human diseases. A Scottish team has genetically engineered sheep that produce milk containing a **protein** used to treat emphysema, a killer lung disease. In the early 1990s, a single sheep called Tracy was already making 1,000th of the entire world output of the drug.

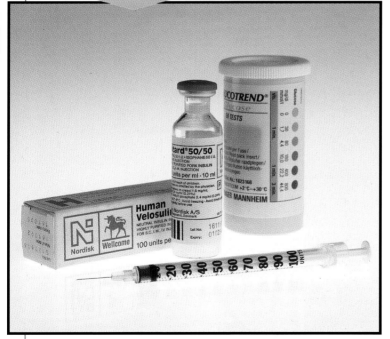

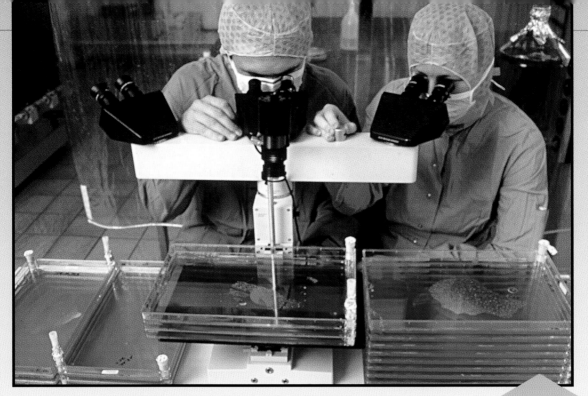

Vaccines—treatments that help prevent an illness from developing by making the body build up an immunity against it—have been used for many years to prevent diseases such as polio, diphtheria, and measles. They are, however, expensive and time-consuming to make. With the aid of genetic engineering these vaccines will be both cheaper and quicker to produce.

Gene therapy

Gene therapy is already offering exciting prospects for treating inherited conditions such as **cystic fibrosis.** By introducing healthy genes into the body cells most affected by the disease—in the case of cystic fibrosis that is the cells of the lungs—it may become possible to correct the disease.

Gene therapy could also be used to correct a person's genetic makeup even before they are born. This has been tried on mice, but not on humans. Many people worry about the possible side effects this form of treatment could have on future generations.

Laboratory researchers wearing protective clothing examine cell cultures through a microscope. The cells have had part of their original **DNA** removed and fresh DNA inserted to make them produce a protein that can be harvested for use in medicines.

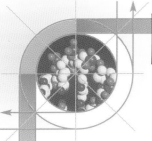

Bioengineering Today

The food we eat

Medicine is only one area that **genetic engineering** will affect. Another is the food we eat. Food can be genetically modified by removing **genes** regarded as harmful, for instance genes that make vegetables go bad. These engineered vegetables could remain on supermarket shelves for much longer, thus reducing waste and increasing profits. Scientists have already tried putting genes from a fish of the flounder family that lives in very cold waters into tomatoes in the hope of making them more resistant to frost.

Farmers plant rice in southern China. Supporters of genetically modified foods claim that they will help produce more abundant crops—an important benefit for a nation like China with more than a billion people to feed.

Those in favor

Those in favor of genetically modified food claim that it will produce better, more reliable crops that will help feed the world's population, which is growing at a staggering 80 million every year. Several large agricultural companies already have succeeded in developing genetically engineered crops. They have produced potatoes that are poisonous to the Colorado beetle—an insect that can damage potato crops and is expensive to get rid of with pesticides.

Corn has been engineered to be resistant to a herbicide, allowing farmers to spray their corn crops and kill the surrounding weeds but not the corn.

Those against

Other people are alarmed by the idea of genetically altered food. Many fear there might be unforeseen long-term consequences to human health as a result of eating such foods. They also worry that once crops are out in the fields, they cannot easily be recalled. If the genetic agents turn out to have unwanted side effects, it might be almost impossible to get rid of them. There are also concerns about possible ripple effects. If a bug-resistant crop is developed and all the bugs go away or starve, then what happens to the birds and other insects that used to eat those bugs?

Bioengineers argue that, far from damaging the environment, the new science offers many possibilities for improving the world around us. Gene engineers are already working on biological cleaning tools that could mop up oil spills in the ocean and eat up chemical waste. There are even plans under way to turn garbage into fuel to power factories and cars.

A researcher examines a crop of corn plants, some of which have been genetically modified so that they can be sprayed with a weed killer. The dead weeds show up brown under the modified plants.

A Fearful Responsibility

Health, profits, and animal rights

Imagine having new hearts to replace faulty ones, **genes** that could help fight cancer, and other genes that could repair damaged brain **cells.** All of these ideas sound great, but the way in which scientists are bringing them about can seem less pleasing. The hearts would be grown in pigs and transferred to humans by surgery, the new brain cells would come from mice, and the knowledge to fight cancer would come at the expense of animals **genetically engineered** to develop the disease.

Pharmaceutical companies conduct such research because they want to find cures for diseases and because they want to make money. Concern over profits may lead to treatments being so expensive that only people in rich countries could afford them.

The world's first genetically engineered monkey, produced to promote research into human diseases, looks to an uncertain future. Animal rights activists worry that medical advances achieved in this manner might be made at an unacceptable cost in suffering to the animals themselves.

The question of cloning

In the strange new world of biogenetics, excitement about new prospects often goes hand-in-hand with worries about the methods used to achieve them. The doubts stretch to **cloning**—creating identical copies of animals or human beings. Scientists proved it could be done in 1996 when they produced Dolly the sheep, in effect the identical twin of her own, six-year-old mother. In theory, people could also be cloned, but research on human cloning is banned in most countries.

One major reason comes from the experiments on Dolly. She was only successfully bred on the 277th attempt. There are strong objections to permitting such lengthy experiments to create human babies.

Many people, too, question why humans would want to produce identical copies of themselves. They also worry about taking steps to "improve" human children. Before long, doctors may be able to remove the genes for inherited diseases from babies before they are born. It may also become possible to alter babies' genes for other reasons—to give them hair of a particular color, for instance, or to make them smarter. Many people object to interfering with nature this way.

The possibilities Crick and Watson opened up on that day in 1953 are impressive. They promise to give people powers over life processes that they previously could not imagine having. Scientists in the next few years will be creating new life-forms and altering those that already exist. The big question is whether people will be able to agree on what scientists should or should not do with that power.

Scientists already possess the techniques necessary to clone human beings, though only at severe risk to the babies' health. For this and other reasons, research on human cloning is prohibited in most countries. This newborn baby was born naturally.

Timeline

400 B.C.E.	Hippocrates, ancient Greece's "father of medicine," suggests that fathers and mothers contribute equal parts of their children's **heredity**
1000 C.E.	Hindu physicians observe that certain diseases run in families
1665	Using the microscope, a recent invention, English scientist Robert Hooke observes and names **cells**
1865	Gregor Mendel publishes the first detailed study of the way in which hereditary traits are passed down
1869	Swiss biologist Johann Friedrich Miescher first observes DNA, calling it "nuclein"
1882	Walther Flemming observes what would later be called **"chromosomes"** and describes how they combine in reproduction
1883	August Weismann suggests that "chromosomes" must be the bearers of heredity
1887	Edouard van Beneden discovers that each species of plant and animal has a fixed number of "chromosomes" in its cells
1902	Walter Sutton coins the word *genes* to describe the factors that carry heredity
1910	T.H. Morgan proves that genes are carried on *chromosomes*
1912	Lawrence Bragg develops **x-ray crystallography**
1944	Oswald Avery shows that DNA can transform organisms, suggesting it might be the bearer of genes
1953	Francis Crick and James D. Watson work out the structure of DNA
1961–65	Genetic code is cracked
1962	Crick, Watson, and Maurice Wilkins win the **Nobel Prize** for Medicine
1977	The first human gene is **cloned**
1982	Genetically engineered insulin is approved for use in treating diabetes in humans
1987	The first genetically engineered microorganisms are used in field experiments
1988	The U.S. Patent Office grants the world's first patent on a mammal—a breed of mice biologically engineered to be likely to develop cancer
1990	The Human Genome Project is launched to locate and identify all the genes in the human body Gene therapy is used for the first time, on a four-year-old American girl with an inherited immune-system disorder. The U.K. bans research into human cloning
1996	Dolly the sheep becomes world's first cloned mammal
1998	A 1-millimeter-long threadworm is the first creature to have its DNA read completely
2000	First draft of the complete human genome is published

Glossary

atom smallest particle of a substance

base in genetics, one of four chemicals in DNA that carry genetic information. The bases are adenine, cytosine, guanine, and thymine.

bioengineering genetic techniques to alter living things

biotechnology techniques used by researchers to change life-forms and produce new organisms

cell microscopic structure that makes up plants and animals

chromosome tiny package of DNA; there are 23 pairs of chromosomes in each human cell

clone to create an identical genetic copy of an animal or plant

crossbreed to bring different strains of animal or plant together for breeding purposes; a mule is crossbred from a horse and a donkey

cystic fibrosis hereditary disease affecting mainly the lungs and pancreas

diabetic person suffering from a disorder that, if untreated, leads to increased levels of sugar in the blood

DNA threadlike material from which genes are made; short for deoxyribonucleic acid

DNA fingerprinting using DNA for identification purposes, in the same way that fingerprints have traditionally been used by police

gene length of DNA carrying instructions to make proteins

genetic engineering methods used by scientists to change the genes found in the cells of all living things

helix structure similar to a spiral

heredity passing on of characteristics from parents to children through the action of the genes

molecule tiny particle, made up of two or more atoms bonded together

muscular dystrophy wasting disease that affects the muscles

Nobel Prize one of the yearly prizes awarded for outstanding achievement in physics, chemistry, medicine, literature, and the promotion of peace

nucleus (plural: nuclei) part of a cell that controls the cell's activity and contains the genes

pharmaceutical describes organizations that make medicines

protein large molecules, made to genes' instructions, that are the basic building blocks of all living things

selective breeding breeding from selected plants or animals to produce improved stock

x-ray crystallography passing x-rays through crystals to create photographic images—a technique that allows scientists to study things like atoms that are too small to be seen by the human eye

Further Reading

Balkwill, Fran. *DNA Is Here to Stay*. Minneapolis, Minn.: Lerner Publishing Group, 1993.

Casanellas, Antonio. *Great Discoveries and Inventions that Improved Human Health*. Milwaukee, Wis.: Gareth Stevens, Inc., 2000.

Stanley, Debbie. *Genetic Engineering: The Cloning Debate*. New York, N.Y.: Rosen Publishing Group, 2000.

Index